Cool
Family Fashions

Keep your loved ones feeling warm and looking cool in cozy designs knit with Bernat® Softee® Chunky™ yarn. This stylish collection features easy cowls, hats, an ear warmer, scarves, hand mitts, and boot cuffs — all designed to chase away winter chills!

About Spinrite:

Established in 1952, Spinrite LP is North America's largest craft yarn producer. Its well-known brands include Patons, Bernat, Caron, and Lily Sugar 'n Cream. For more about Spinrite, visit Yarnspirations.com, a one-stop resource for everything that you need to create knit and crochet projects to suit any mood, budget, or occasion.

LEISURE ARTS, INC. • Maumelle, Arkansas

Ear Warmer

■■□□ **EASY +**

Finished Size: 6" wide x 22" long (15.25 cm x 56 cm)

SHOPPING LIST

Yarn (Super Bulky Weight)
Bernat® Softee® Chunky™
[3.5 ounces, 108 yards
(100 grams, 99 meters) per skein]:
☐ #28417 Peony Pink - 1 skein

Knitting Needles
☐ Straight, size 11 (8 mm)
   or size needed for gauge

Additional Supplies
☐ 1⅝" (41 mm) Button
☐ Yarn needle

GAUGE INFORMATION

In pattern,
   15 sts = 6" (15.25 cm)

TECHNIQUES USED

· YO *(Fig. 4, page 44)*
· K2 tog *(Fig. 5, page 44)*
· P3 tog *(Fig. 7, page 45)*
· SSK *(Figs. 8a-c, page 46)*

INSTRUCTIONS

Cast on 15 sts.

Rows 1-3: Knit across.

Row 4 (Right side)**:** K2, SSK twice, YO, (K1, YO) 3 times, K2 tog twice, K2.

Row 5: K2, P 11, K2.

Row 6: Knit across.

Row 7: K2, P 11, K2.

Repeat Rows 4-7 for pattern until piece measures approximately 19" (48.5 cm) from cast on edge **or** 3" (7.5 cm) less than desired length, ending by working Row 5.

SHAPING

Row 1: K2, SSK, K7, K2 tog, K2: 13 sts.

Row 2: K2, P9, K2.

Row 3: K2, SSK twice, YO, K1, YO, K2 tog twice, K2: 11 sts.

Row 4: K2, P7, K2.

Row 5: K2, SSK, K3, K2 tog, K2: 9 sts.

Row 6: K2, P5, K2.

Row 7: K2, SSK, K1, K2 tog, K2: 7 sts.

Row 8: K2, P3 tog, K2: 5 sts.

Row 9 (Buttonhole row)**:** K1, K2 tog, YO, K2: 5 sts.

Row 10: Knit across.

Row 11: SSK, K1, K2 tog: 3 sts.

Bind off remaining sts in **knit**.

Sew button to center of Ear Warmer, 2¹/₂" (6.5 cm) from cast on edge.

Boot Cuffs

■□□□ **BEGINNER**

——— SHOPPING LIST ———

Yarn (Super Bulky Weight)

Bernat® Softee® Chunky™

[3.5 ounces, 108 yards

(100 grams, 99 meters) per skein]:

☐ #28705 Berry Red - 1 skein

Knitting Needles

☐ Straight, size 11 (8 mm)

   or size needed for gauge

Additional Supplies

☐ Yarn needle

SIZE INFORMATION

Finished Circumference:

Small - 11¼" (28.5 cm)

Medium - 12¾" (32.5 cm)

Large - 14½" (37 cm)

Size Note: We have printed the instructions for the sizes in different colors to make it easier for you to find:

· Small in Blue

· Medium in Pink

· Large in Green

Instructions in Black apply to all sizes.

GAUGE INFORMATION

In pattern,

  10 sts and 15 rows = 4"

  (10 cm)

INSTRUCTIONS

Cast on 30{34-38} sts.

Row 1: P2, (K1, P1) across.

Row 2 (Right side)**:** Knit across.

Repeat Rows 1 and 2 for pattern until Boot Cuff measures approximately 5{5½-6}"/12.5{14-15} cm from cast on edge, ending by working Row 1.

Bind off all sts in **knit** leaving a long end for sewing.

Fold the Cuff in half with the **right** side facing you and matching the ends of the rows. Using the long end, weave the edges together *(Fig. 9, page 47)*.

Repeat for second Boot Cuff.

Eyelet Scarf

■■□□ EASY

Finished Size: 5¹/₂" wide x 72" long (14 cm x 183 cm)
Note: The Scarf can be worked to any length.
The model shown on page 13 is 55" (139.5 cm) long.

──── SHOPPING LIST ────

Yarn (Super Bulky Weight)
Bernat® Softee® Chunky™

[3.5 ounces, 108 yards
(100 grams, 99 meters) per skein]:
☐ #28307 Lavender - 2 skeins
OR

[2.8 ounces, 77 yards
(80 grams, 70 meters) per skein]:
☐ #29117 Stillness Ombre - 2 skeins

Knitting Needles

☐ Straight, size 11 (8 mm)
or size needed for gauge

GAUGE INFORMATION

In pattern, 13 sts = 5½" (14 cm)

TECHNIQUES USED

· YO *(Fig. 4, page 44)*
· K2 tog *(Fig. 5, page 44)*

INSTRUCTIONS

Cast on 13 sts.

Rows 1-3: Knit across.

Row 4: (K2, YO, K2 tog) 3 times, K1.

Rows 5-7: Knit across.

Row 8: K4, YO, K2 tog, K2, YO, K2 tog, K3.

Repeat Rows 1-8 for pattern until Scarf measures approximately 72" (183 cm) from cast on edge **or** to desired length, ending by working Row 7.

Bind off all sts in **knit**.

Hand Mitts

■□□□ **BEGINNER**

── SHOPPING LIST ──

Yarn (Super Bulky Weight)

Bernat® Softee® Chunky™

[3.5 ounces, 108 yards
(100 grams, 99 meters) per skein]:

☐ Color A, #28607 Glowing Gold - 1 skein

☐ Color B, #28044 True Grey - 1 skein

Knitting Needles

☐ Straight, size 11 (8 mm)
   or size needed for gauge

Additional Supplies

☐ Yarn needle

SIZE INFORMATION

Finished Hand Circumference:

Small - 6¹/₂" (16.5 cm)

Medium - 8" (20.5 cm)

Large - 8³/₄" (22 cm)

Size Note: We have printed the instructions for the sizes in different colors to make it easier for you to find:

· Small in Blue

· Medium in Pink

· Large in Green

Instructions in Black apply to all sizes.

GAUGE INFORMATION

In Stockinette Stitch (knit one row, purl one row),

10 sts = 4" (10 cm)

INSTRUCTIONS

WRIST RIBBING

Using Color A and leaving a long end for sewing, cast on 18{22-24} sts.

Row 1: (K1, P1) across.

Loop a short piece of yarn around the last stitch made.

Repeat Row 1 until Wrist Ribbing measures approximately 2" (5 cm), ending at marked edge; cut Color A.

BODY

Using Color B and beginning with a **knit** row, work in Stockinette Stitch (knit one row, purl one row) until piece measures approximately 4{5-6}"/10{12.5-15} cm from cast on edge.

TOP RIBBING

Row 1: (K1, P1) across; cut Color B.

Row 2: Using Color A, (K1, P1) across.

Repeat Row 2 until Top Ribbing measures approximately 2" (5 cm).

Bind off all sts in ribbing leaving a long end for sewing.

FINISHING

Fold the Hand Mitt with the **right** side facing you and matching the ends of the rows. Using the first long end, weave the Wrist Ribbing and the Body for the first 2^1/$_2${2^3/$_4$-3}"/ 6.5{7-7.5} cm *(Fig. 9, page 47)*.

Using the second yarn end, weave the Top Ribbing and the Body for 2^1/$_4${2^3/$_4$-3}"/ 5.5{7-7.5} cm, leaving a 1^1/$_4${1^1/$_2$-2}"/3{4-5} cm opening for the thumb opening.

Repeat for second Hand Mitt.

Hooded Scarf

 **EASY**

——— SHOPPING LIST ———

Yarn (Super Bulky Weight)
Bernat® Softee® Chunky™
[3.5 ounces, 108 yards
(100 grams, 99 meters) per skein]:
☐ #28342 Teal Twists - 3 skeins

Knitting Needles
☐ Straight, size 13 (9 mm)
   or size needed for gauge

Additional Supplies
☐ Yarn needle

SIZE INFORMATION

Finished Hood Width:

Small - 17$^{1}/_{2}$" (44.5 cm)

Medium/Large - 22$^{1}/_{2}$" (57 cm)

Size Note: We have printed the instructions for the sizes in different colors to make it easier for you to find:

· Small in Blue

· Medium/Large in Pink

Instructions in Black apply to both sizes.

GAUGE INFORMATION

In pattern,

12 sts (2 repeats) = 5"

(12.75 cm),

15 rows = 4" (10 cm)

TECHNIQUE USED

· Adding sts *(Figs. 3a & b, page 43)*

INSTRUCTIONS

FIRST SIDE

Cast on 16 sts.

Rows 1 and 2: Knit across.

Row 3: P4, (K2, P4) twice.

Row 4 (Right side)**:** Knit across.

Row 5: P1, K2, (P4, K2) twice, K1.

Row 6: Knit across.

Repeat Rows 3-6 for pattern until First Side measures approximately 20{25^1/$_2$}"/51{65} cm from cast on edge, ending by working Row 5.

HOOD
Row 1: Add on 6{12} sts, knit across: 22{28} sts.

Repeat Rows 3-6 of First Scarf until Hood measures approximately 17^1/$_2${19}"/44.5{48.5} cm from added on sts, ending by working Row 5.

SECOND SIDE
Row 1: Bind off 6{12} sts, knit across: 16 sts.

Repeat Rows 3-6 of First Side until Second Side measures same as First Side, ending by working Row 5.

Last 2 Rows: Knit across.

Bind off all sts in **knit**.

Fold the Hood in half with the **right** side facing you and matching the bound off sts to the added on sts. Weave the back Hood seam across the ends of the rows from the bottom edge of the Hood to the fold *(Fig. 9, page 47)*.

Lace Hat

■■□□ **EASY +**

SHOPPING LIST

Yarn (Super Bulky Weight) SUPER BULKY 6

Bernat® Softee® Chunky™

[3.5 ounces, 108 yards
(100 grams, 99 meters) per skein]:

☐ #28418 Baby Pink - 1 skein

Knitting Needle

☐ 16" (40.5 cm) Circular, size 11 (8 mm)
or size needed for gauge

Additional Supplies

☐ Marker
☐ Yarn needle

GAUGE INFORMATION

In Body pattern,

10 sts and 20 rnds = 4"
(10 cm)

TECHNIQUES USED

· Knit tbl *(Fig. 2, page 43)*
· YO *(Fig. 4, page 44)*
· K2 tog *(Fig. 5, page 44)*
· SSK *(Figs. 8a-c, page 46)*

INSTRUCTIONS
BRIM

Cast on 42{48} sts *(see Using A Circular Needle, page 42)*; place marker to indicate the beginning of the round *(see Markers, page 41)*.

Rnds 1-4: Knit around.

Rnd 5: (YO, K2 tog) around.

Rnd 6: (K1 tbl, K1) around.

Rnds 7-9: Knit around.

SIZE INFORMATION

Finished Brim Circumference:
Small - 16³/₄" (42.5 cm)
Medium - 19¹/₄" (49 cm)

Size Note: We have printed the instructions for the sizes in different colors to make it easier for you to find:
· Small in Blue
· Medium in Pink
Instructions in Black apply to both sizes.

Rnd 10: To form Brim, lift up the bottom edge toward the inside. Matching cast on sts with sts on last rnd, ★ insert right needle through next st **and** through cast on st, knitting them together as one st to join edges *(Fig. A)*; repeat from ★ around.

Fig. A

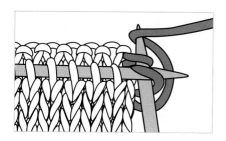

BODY

Rnd 1: Knit around.

Rnd 2: Purl around.

Rnd 3: Knit around.

Rnd 4: (YO, SSK) around.

Rnd 5: (K1 tbl, K1) around.

Rnd 6: Purl around.

Rnd 7: Knit around.

Rnd 8: (YO, K2 tog) around.

Rnd 9: (K1 tbl, K1) around.

Repeat Rnds 2-9 for lace pattern until Hat measures approximately 7{8}"/18{20.5} cm from folded edge, ending by working Rnd 3.

Cut yarn leaving an 18" (45.5 cm) length for sewing.

Thread yarn needle with long end and slip sts onto yarn needle; gather tightly to close and secure end.

Design by Kathy Norris.

Ridged Cowl

◧■□▷ **EASY**

Finished Size: 17" wide x 21" circumference (43 cm x 53.5 cm)

── SHOPPING LIST ──

Yarn (Super Bulky Weight)
Bernat® Softee® Chunky™
[3.5 ounces, 108 yards
(100 grams, 99 meters) per skein]:
☐ Color A, #28008 Natural - 1 skein
☐ Color B, #28041 Clay - 1 skein

Knitting Needles
☐ Straight, size 15 (10 mm)
or size needed for gauge

Additional Supplies
☐ Yarn needle

GAUGE INFORMATION

In pattern,

    9 sts = 4" (10 cm),

    18 rows = $4^1/_4$" (10.75 cm)

INSTRUCTIONS

With Color A, cast on 38 sts.

Row 1 (Right side)**:** Knit across.

Rows 2-4: Purl across.

Row 5: Knit across.

Rows 6 and 7: Purl across.

Row 8: Knit across.

Rows 9 and 10: Purl across.

Rows 11-13: Knit across.

Row 14: Purl across.

Rows 15 and 16: Knit across.

Row 17: Purl across.

Row 18: Knit across.

Rows 19-45: Repeat Rows 1-18 once, then repeat Rows 1-9 once **more**.

Rows 46-54: Cut Color A; with Color B, repeat Rows 10-18.

Rows 55-90: Repeat Rows 1-18 twice.

Bind off all sts in **knit** leaving a long end for sewing.

Fold piece in half matching cast on edge to bound off edge. Using long end, weave edges together as follows:

Bring the needle from behind the work and through the center of the first stitch on the bottom piece. ★ Insert the needle behind both loops of the next stitch on the top piece *(Fig. A)*. Insert the needle behind both loops of the inverted V of the next stitch on the bottom piece. Repeat from ★ across. Pull the yarn gently every 2 or 3 stitches, being careful to maintain even tension.

Fig. A

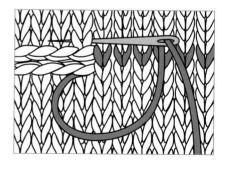

Design by Lisa Gentry.

Slouch Hat

■■□▷ EASY +

── SHOPPING LIST ──

Yarn (Super Bulky Weight)

Bernat® Softee® Chunky™
[3.5 ounces, 108 yards
(100 grams, 99 meters) per skein]:
- ☐ #28200 Emerald - 2 skeins

Knitting Needles
16" (40.5 cm) Circular,
- ☐ Size 11 (8 mm) **and**
- ☐ Size 15 (10 mm),

Double pointed (set of 4),
- ☐ Size 15 (10 mm)

   or sizes needed for gauge

Additional Supplies
- ☐ Split ring marker
- ☐ Yarn needle

GAUGE INFORMATION

In Twisted Garter Stitch (purl one rnd, knit tbl one rnd), with smaller size needle,
  10 sts = 4" (10 cm)
In Twisted Stockinette Stitch (knit tbl every rnd), with larger size needle,
  10 sts and 12 rows = 4" (10 cm)

Note: Since the Twisted Stockinette Stitch is a tighter stitch than the Twisted Garter Stitch, you will need a different needle size for each pattern stitch to maintain the same stitch gauge.

SIZE INFORMATION

Finished Band Circumference:
Small - 16" (40.5 cm)
Medium - 19¹/₄" (49 cm)

Size Note: We have printed the instructions for the sizes in different colors to make it easier for you to find:
· Small in Blue
· Medium in Pink
Instructions in Black apply to both sizes.

TECHNIQUES USED
· Knit tbl *(Fig. 2, page 43)*
· K2 tog *(Fig. 5, page 44)*
· K2 tog tbl *(Fig. 6, page 45)*

——— STITCH GUIDE ———
INCREASE
Insert the right needle from the **front** into the side of the stitch **below** the next stitch on the left needle *(Fig. A)* and knit it.

Fig. A

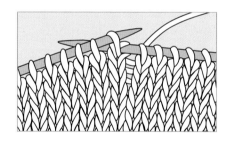

INSTRUCTIONS
BAND
Using smaller size needle, cast on 40{48} sts *(see Using A Circular Needle, page 42)*; place marker to indicate the beginning of the round *(see Markers, page 41)*.

Rnd 1: Purl around.

Rnd 2: Knit tbl around.

Rnds 3 thru 10{12}: Repeat Rnds 1 and 2, 4{5} times.

BODY

Change to larger size circular needle.

Rnds 1-3: Knit tbl around.

Rnd 4: K3 tbl, increase, K2 tbl, increase, ★ K6 tbl, increase, K2 tbl, increase; repeat from ★ around to last 3 sts, K3 tbl: 50{60} sts.

Rnd 5: Knit tbl around.

Rnd 6: K4 tbl, increase, K2 tbl, increase, ★ K8 tbl, increase, K2 tbl, increase; repeat from ★ around to last 4 sts, K4 tbl: 60{72} sts.

Rnd 7: Knit tbl around.

Rnd 8: K5 tbl, increase, K2 tbl, increase, ★ K 10 tbl, increase, K2 tbl, increase; repeat from ★ around to last 5 sts, K5 tbl: 70{84} sts.

Rnds 9 thru 17{21}: Knit tbl around.

Rnd 18{22}: K5 tbl, K2 tog, K2 tog tbl, ★ K 10 tbl, K2 tog, K2 tog tbl; repeat from ★ around to last 5 sts, K5 tbl: 60{72} sts.

Rnd 19{23}: Knit tbl around.

Rnd 20{24}: K4 tbl, K2 tog, K2 tog tbl, ★ K8 tbl, K2 tog, K2 tog tbl; repeat from ★ around to last 4 sts, K4 tbl: 50{60} sts.

Rnd 21{25}: Knit tbl around.

Divide the stitches evenly between 3 double pointed needles. Use the remaining needle to work across the stitches on the first needle. You will then have an empty needle with which to work the stitches from the next needle. Work the first stitch of each needle firmly to prevent gaps.

Rnd 22{26}: K3 tbl, K2 tog, K2 tog tbl, ★ K6 tbl, K2 tog, K2 tog tbl; repeat from ★ around to last 3 sts, K3 tbl: 40{48} sts.

Rnd 23{27}: Knit tbl around.

Rnd 24{28}: K2 tbl, K2 tog, K2 tog tbl, ★ K4 tbl, K2 tog, K2 tog tbl; repeat from ★ around to last 2 sts, K2 tbl: 30{36} sts.

Rnd 25{29}: Knit tbl around.

Rnd 26{30}: K1 tbl, K2 tog, K2 tog tbl, ★ K2 tbl, K2 tog, K2 tog tbl; repeat from ★ around to last st, K1 tbl: 20{24} sts.

Rnd 27{31}: Knit tbl around.

Rnd 28{32}: K2 tog tbl around; cut yarn leaving a long end for sewing: 10{12} sts.

Thread yarn needle with long end and slip remaining sts onto yarn needle; gather tightly to close and secure end.

Design by Kathy Norris.

Waffle Stitch Cowl

■■□□ EASY **+**

Finished Size: 13" high x 27¹/₂"
circumference (33 cm x 70 cm)

— SHOPPING LIST —

Yarn (Super Bulky Weight)
Bernat® Softee® Chunky™
[2.8 ounces, 77 yards
(80 grams, 70 meters) per skein]:
☐ #29121 Shadow Ombre - 2 skeins

Knitting Needle

24" (61 cm) Circular,
☐ Size 15 (10 mm)
 or size needed for gauge

Additional Supplies

☐ Marker

GAUGE INFORMATION

In pattern,

   9 sts and 12 rnds = 3³/₄"
   (9.5 cm)

INSTRUCTIONS

Cast on 66 sts *(see Using A Circular Needle, page 42)*; place marker to indicate the beginning of the round *(see Markers, page 41)*.

Rnds 1-6: (K1, P1) around.

Rnds 7-9: (K2, P1) around.

Rnd 10: Purl around.

Repeat Rnds 7-10 for pattern until Cowl measures approximately 11" (28 cm) from cast on edge **or** 2" (5 cm) less than desired height, ending by working Rnd 9.

Last 6 Rnds: (K1, P1) around.

Bind off all sts in pattern.

General Instructions

ABBREVIATIONS

cm	centimeters
K	knit
mm	millimeters
P	purl
Rnd(s)	Round(s)
SSK	slip, slip, knit
st(s)	stitch(es)
tbl	through back loop
tog	together
YO	yarn over

SYMBOLS & TERMS

★ — work instructions following ★ as many **more** times as indicated in addition to the first time.

( ) or [ ] — work enclosed instructions **as many** times as specified by the number immediately following **or** contains explanatory remarks.

colon (:) — the number(s) given after a colon at the end of a row or round denote(s) the number of stitches you should have on that row or round.

KNIT TERMINOLOGY	
UNITED STATES	**INTERNATIONAL**
gauge =	tension
bind off =	cast off
yarn over (YO) =	yarn forward (yfwd) **or** yarn around needle (yrn)

KNITTING NEEDLES		
UNITED STATES	ENGLISH U.K.	METRIC (mm)
0	13	2
1	12	2.25
2	11	2.75
3	10	3.25
4	9	3.5
5	8	3.75
6	7	4
7	6	4.5
8	5	5
9	4	5.5
10	3	6
10½	2	6.5
11	1	8
13	00	9
15	000	10
17	---	12.75
19	---	15
35	---	19
50	---	25

Yarn Weight Symbol & Names	LACE 0	SUPER FINE 1	FINE 2	LIGHT 3	MEDIUM 4	BULKY 5	SUPER BULKY 6
Type of Yarns in Category	Fingering, size 10 crochet thread	Sock, Fingering, Baby	Sport, Baby	DK, Light Worsted	Worsted, Afghan, Aran	Chunky, Craft, Rug	Bulky, Roving
Knit Gauge Range* in Stockinette St to 4" (10 cm)	33-40** sts	27-32 sts	23-26 sts	21-24 sts	16-20 sts	12-15 sts	6-11 sts
Advised Needle Size Range	000-1	1 to 3	3 to 5	5 to 7	7 to 9	9 to 11	11 and larger

*GUIDELINES ONLY: The chart above reflects the most commonly used gauges and needle sizes for specific yarn categories.

** Lace weight yarns are usually knitted on larger needles to create lacy openwork patterns. Accordingly, a gauge range is difficult to determine. Always follow the gauge stated in your pattern.

GAUGE

Exact gauge is essential for proper size or fit. Before beginning your project, make a sample swatch in the yarn and needle specified in the individual instructions. After completing the swatch, measure it, counting your stitches and rows carefully. If your swatch is larger or smaller than specified, **make another, changing needle size to get the correct gauge**. Keep trying until you find the size needles that will give you the specified gauge.

MARKERS

As a convenience to you, we have used markers to mark the beginning of a round. Place markers as instructed. You may use a purchased marker or tie a length of contrasting color yarn around the needle. When you reach the marker on each round, slip it from the left needle to the right needle; remove it when no longer needed.

When using double pointed needles, a split-ring marker can be placed around the first stitch in the round to indicate the beginning of the round. Move it up at the end of each round.

■□□□ BEGINNER	Projects for first-time knitters using basic knit and purl stitches. Minimal shaping.
■■□□ EASY	Projects using basic stitches, repetitive stitch patterns, simple color changes, and simple shaping and finishing.
■■■□ INTERMEDIATE	Projects with a variety of stitches, such as basic cables and lace, simple intarsia, double-pointed needles and knitting in the round needle techniques, mid-level shaping and finishing.
■■■■ EXPERIENCED	Projects using advanced techniques and stitches, such as short rows, fair isle, more intricate intarsia, cables, lace patterns, and numerous color changes.

USING A CIRCULAR NEEDLE

When you knit a tube, you are going to work around on the outside of the circle with the **right** side of the knitting facing you. Using a circular needle, cast on all stitches as instructed. Untwist and straighten the stitches on the needle to be sure that the cast on ridge lays on the inside of the needle and never rolls around the needle.

Hold the needle so that the ball of yarn is attached to the stitch closest to the right hand point. Place a marker on the right hand point to mark the beginning of the round.

To begin working in the round, knit the stitches on the left hand point *(Fig. 1)*. Continue working each round as instructed without turning the work.

Fig. 1

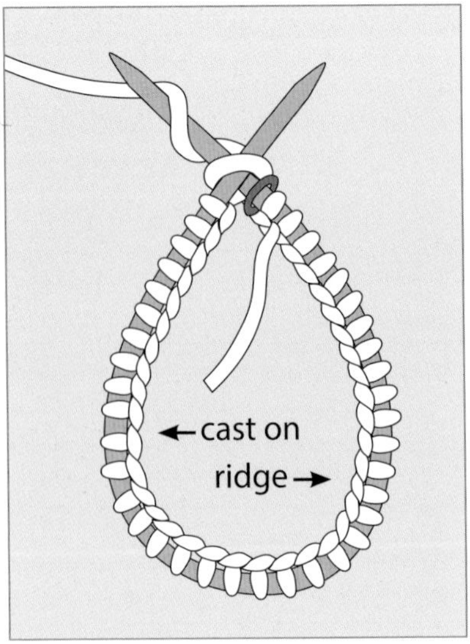

cast on ridge

KNIT THROUGH BACK LOOP (abbreviated knit tbl)

Insert the right needle into the **back** loop of the next stitch (*Fig. 2*), then knit the stitch.

Fig. 2

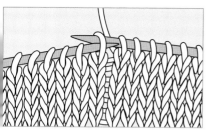

ADDING STITCHES

Insert the right needle into the stitch as if to **knit**, yarn over and pull loop through (*Fig. 3a*), insert left needle into loop just worked from **front** to **back** and slip it onto the left needle (*Fig. 3b*). Repeat for the required number of stitches.

Fig. 3a

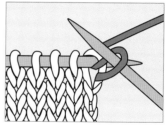

Fig. 3b

YARN OVER

Bring the yarn forward **between** the needles, then back **over** the top of the right hand needle, so that it is now in position to knit the next stitch *(Fig. 4)*.

Fig. 4

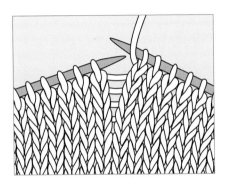

DECREASES
KNIT 2 TOGETHER

(abbreviated K2 tog)

Insert the right needle into the **front** of the first two stitches on the left needle as if to **knit** *(Fig. 5)*, then **knit** them together as if they were one stitch.

Fig. 5

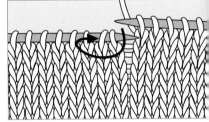

KNIT 2 TOGETHER THROUGH BACK LOOP

(abbreviated K2 tog tbl)

Insert the right needle into the **back** of the first two stitches on the left needle as if to **knit** *(Fig. 6)*, then **knit** them together as if they were one stitch.

Fig. 6

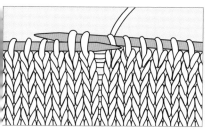

PURL 3 TOGETHER

(abbreviated P3 tog)

Insert the right needle into the **front** of the first three stitches on the left needle as if to **purl** *(Fig. 7)*, then **purl** them together as if they were one stitch.

Fig. 7

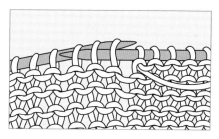

SLIP, SLIP, KNIT *(abbreviated SSK)*

Separately slip two stitches as if to **knit** *(Fig. 8a)*. Insert the left needle into the **front** of both slipped stitches *(Fig. 8b)* and then **knit** them together as if they were one stitch *(Fig. 8c)*.

Fig. 8a

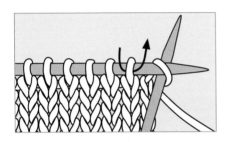

Fig. 8b

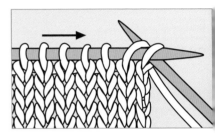

Fig. 8c

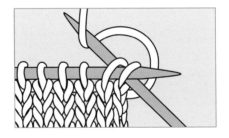

WEAVING SEAMS

With the **right** side of both sides facing you and edges even, sew through both sides once to secure the beginning of the seam. Insert the needle under the bar between the first and second stitches on the row and pull the yarn through *(Fig. 9)*. Insert the needle under the next bar on the second side. Repeat from side to side, being careful to match rows. If the edges are different lengths, it may be necessary to insert the needle under two bars at one edge.

Fig. 9

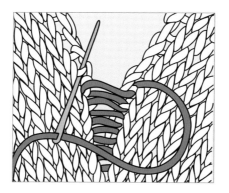

We have made every effort to ensure that these instructions are accurate and complete. We cannot, however, be responsible for human error, typographical mistakes, or variations in individual work.

Production Team: Writer/Technical Editor - Cathy Hardy; Editorial Writer - Susan Frantz Wiles; Senior Graphic Artist - Lora Puls; Graphic Artist - Jessica Bramlett; Photo Stylist - Lori Wenger; and Photographer - Jason Masters.

Instructions tested and photo models made by Lee Ellis and Raymelle Greening.